100 WAYS
TO TEACH YOUR
CHILD TO READ

100 WAYS TO TEACH YOUR CHILD TO READ

A Guide for Parents and Teachers

Tissua S. Franklin

gatekeeper press
Tampa, Florida

100 Ways to Teach Your Child to Read:
A Guide for Parents and Teachers

Published by Gatekeeper Press
7853 Gunn Hwy., Suite 209
Tampa, FL 33626
www.GatekeeperPress.com

Library of Congress Control Number: 2023938963

ISBN (paperback): 9781662940590
eISBN: 9781662940606

*This book is dedicated to
all the children who didn't learn, haven't learned,
or won't learn how to read due to grown-ups' oversight
of the importance of it. I'm sorry.*

FOREWORD

The book was written because of information I discovered concerning Detroit's public-school children. Only 1% of Detroit's children are prepared for kindergarten and only 10% are reading by third grade. A new reading law was put into place stating any child not reading at level by third grade would fail third grade. In Detroit, that could be as many as 3,000 students. That is a tragedy.

In inner cities where children are not given equal educational opportunities, it seems as if no one is paying attention. For years, these children have been overlooked and many have gone from school to prison. Those children who do not get a proper education often end up dead or in jail. This book is to help parents set a foundation for their child and ensure they can read by third grade. All these strategies are tried-and-true and have stood the test of time.

You may adjust any of these strategies and make them digital using your creativity.

If you check out my YouTube channel you can get a REAL idea of what it feels like to work with children. It does not always go as planned. You can adjust as needed and some days you can just stop. Children have ups and downs, just like adults, and every day is not a focused learning day. However, I press on and forward most times, and even extend the learning time if they are having a good day. Don't stress too much, especially when trying a new activity. It won't always go well, but with persistence and routine your child will become a better reader, I promise.

For questions, concerns, or next steps, please feel free to contact me at **purposefuleducations.com** or **purposefuleducations@gmail.com.**

100 WAYS TO TEACH YOUR CHILD TO READ

Parents are a child's first teacher. Every day we model and demonstrate for our children. From us, they are learning what is important, and what is not; how to be good decision-makers, or not; and how to behave in good and bad situations.

It's true we are "training up" our children. The apple doesn't fall from the tree. In some cases, our children grow up to be our "mini-ME's."

I say that to say this, if you want reading to be important, you must make it important. That means you must model and demonstrate when you read, why you read, and discuss why it is important, with your learner.

I also want to mention, "You have the power of life and death in your tongue." Your children are going to be what you say they will be. Speak life into them! Tell them they are good.

Thank them for using good words, for sharing, and being kind to others.

Tell them they are smart, pretty, or handsome, and that they can be whatever they want to be.

Give to your children—not just expensive material gifts—but give them intrinsic rewards. For example, give hugs, movie nights, and family fun days. Tell them you love them, then back it up with family dinner nights where you cook together. Give them swimming or piano lessons. Allow them to be a part of a sports program and come watch them play the game. Spend time reading books and visiting the library. Send love notes in their lunches or sneak them into their bookbags. I still do this, and my children are twenty and twenty-four.

The strategies in this book can be used in your home or in a classroom. I have shared these activities with children who are struggling readers and writers, have special needs, are bilingual, or gifted. These activities are meant to help you give your learner the foundational skills needed to grow academically. I hope you enjoy doing these activities with your learners as much as I enjoy doing them with learners. Please send me pictures of a-ha moments. I feel a sequel coming on as your children grow and learn more and more.

Let's start with how to make reading important in your home. You can start by creating a print-rich environment.

Creating a print-rich environment means creating an environment full of print that is used for many different purposes. This includes signs, posters, magazines, menus, books, lists, poems, words, pictures, and newspapers. It is recommended to display words in two languages, especially if you are bilingual. There are many ways to purposefully create a print-rich environment in your home. Here are a few:

Print-Enriched Environment

1

Put into writing things that are relevant to your child and display them around the house and in their room. Remember to read them frequently and refer to them whenever convenient. For example, norms for learning time, toothbrushing steps, menus, or bedtime routines.

Add pictures to go with the rules; this will support their learning. Once they have learned the words you can remove the pictures. Below is just one example of norms for learning in my class.

Norms for Learning
- Say, "I can!"
- Try your best.
- Share with others.

Read these together whenever possible. That is the "use it" part. For a print-rich environment to provide a reading strategy that works, you must use the print in the environment in meaningful ways.

2

Create a print-rich environment by hanging the alphabet with pictures if you plan for this to aid in their reading. Be consistent! Hang color words, number words, months of the year, days of the week, number charts, and shapes. You may even create a calendar area. Again, you can't just hang these things up; you must use them in a routine as often as possible. Check out my YouTube for what the calendar can look like.

3 ....

Create a print-rich environment by labeling items around the house, or in their room, at minimum. Examples: mirror, door, desk, chair, closet, and window.

4 ....

Use a portion of their bedroom wall to create a mini word wall. Add high-frequency words as you teach them. Start this wall with their first and last name, names of parents and siblings, and places they like to go, like the library, zoo, or McDonald's. Pictures with words are most powerful.

5 ....

Place magazines around the house. Get a subscription to a children's periodical like *Highlights* and *National Geographic Kids*. You can turn their bedroom into a print-rich environment by hanging their work on the wall and posting anchor charts of what they learn.

6 ....

Now that you know a little bit about how to make a print-rich environment, let's talk a bit more about making reading important in your home. Read to your child each night. Make it a priority!

Reading to your child for 15-20 minutes daily is the most effective way to teach your child to read and that reading is important. That tidbit of information is the most useful information in this book and if you use it, you've just paid for this book.

Reading to your child each night has multiple benefits. It teaches them what a fluent reader sounds like; it introduces them to new vocabulary; it lets them know that their thoughts can be put on paper and their imagination can be sparked through a book—and let's not forget reading to learn.

Reading makes children smarter. From before birth to around third grade children are *learning to read*. That means you can read to your child in the womb, and it will have effects years later. After third grade, children are *reading to learn*.

Reading each night for 15-20 minutes will increase your child's standardized test scores, spark their curiosity, and give them a love for reading.

7 ....

Remember to pause and discuss the roles of the author and illustrator. The author writes the story while the illustrator draws the pictures. When they have an opportunity to write, let them know they are performing the job of an author. When they have an opportunity to draw, let them know that they are doing the job of the illustrator.

8 ....

In a narrative story, pause and talk about the main character(s), where the story takes place (setting), what the problem in the story is (conflict) and how the characters may solve it. Discussing characters' names and where the story takes place are lower-level thinking questions. Asking about the problem and how it was solved are examples of higher-level thinking. However, if your child can make reference to other stories' similarities and differences; share how the characters are like someone they know, or like themselves; or be able to use the same situation and problem-solving skills from the book, then they are making connections to real life and that's higher-level thinking skills that we all need.

9 ....

When reading informational books, remember to look at text features such as the table of contents, the glossary, index, subtopics, and subheadings. Discuss what information is shared in each. Discuss the difference between a narrative story and an informational story. Look closely at the pictures in informational text and the information that the author gives in the captions underneath it. Pictures are often a way to get valuable information to struggling readers. You can even write down some of the information learned or have your student draw a picture of something that will remind them of the information they learned.

10 ....

Read poems to your child too. Point out to them that poems can be on different topics. Some poems can be rhyming; really talk about those rhyming poems. Talk about how rhyming words sound the same at the end and how the first part of the word only changes. Make rhyming words together. Write those rhyming words on charts. The chart may say: "cat, hat, bat, rat, sat." Add pictures to go with it. You can talk about haiku, limericks, alliteration, and poems. Children love acrostic poems and can make one with their name.

For example:
Teaching
Is
Super
Satisfying and
Unbelievably
Amazing

11 ....

Read biographies and autobiographies with your child. They are both genres about someone's life story. However, "auto" means "I," which means an autobiography is a story that someone wrote about their own life. A biography is a story that someone else wrote about someone's life.

12 ....

Point out the difference between each genre. A genre is a certain type of book. We do this to show students that there is a difference and the information inside of each will be different. We also want them to know that they can be reading about the same topic using a different genre. For example, learners can learn about dinosaurs by reading a narrative story about dinosaurs, a poem, or an informational story. Visit my YouTube page for examples of a genre poster.

13 ....

Talk about author's point of view. Tell your child that the author is always speaking from a point of view. First-person point of view is the person telling the story and told with words such as "I," "we," "us," or "me." Second-person point of view is when someone is being addressed and uses words such as "you," "yours," or "yourself," while third-person point of view is when someone else is being talked about and pronouns used are "he," "she," "her," "them," or "they." I help my students remember it like this-if I am going to tell a story about something that happened to me, it's in the first person. If I am going to tell a story about you, that's second person. If someone else tells the story about people they don't know, that's third person.

14 ....

Point of view also has to do with who is telling the story and why. Because a story is told from a person's point of view, it's good to learn about the author and why they may have written their book. In informational text it is important to find out if the information is true or not. Are the authors reputable or just giving their opinion? This has to do with comprehension and critical-thinking skills.

15

Talk to your child about purpose. Why do you think the author wrote this book? Is it to entertain us, give us information, or persuade us to do something? What words in the book tell us this?

16

Have your child retell stories you have read and stories from past experiences such as birthdays and family vacations. When retelling stories make sure your child uses characters' names and actual names of places. Have them use transitional words such as "first," "then," "next," and "finally." Since we live in a virtual world, you can take pictures of events such as birthdays and vacations and use these to write stories or verbally retell stories.

17

Sing "The Alphabet Song" both forward and backward. Make sure to separate the letters, especially "l," "m," "n," "o," and "p."

18

Use a set of alphabet cards: mix them up and have your child put them back in order. Teach your child that each letter makes a sound. Do not add /a/ sound to the end of letters. "N" says /n/, not /na/.

19

Use a letter picture chart to help your child. For example: A /a/ alligator, b /b/ bumblebee, c /c/ caterpillar. This is a way to repeat the letter, its sound, and a word that starts with the letter.

20

Use index cards to write the alphabet on and have your child put the letters in order. Use an alphabet chart to support them as they identify each letter and where it belongs. Eventually, you should be able to take the chart away.

21

Use the same index cards from prior suggestion and teach those sounds. Don't use all the letters at once. If your child knows certain sounds already, use those and add three to four new sounds each week, making sure to do activities to help them remember the sounds. I'll mention some activities later. If they don't know a sound, you can teach one or two new sounds each week. There are lots of activities you can use to teach letters. Show your child each letter and teach them to say, "'a' says /a/, 'b' says /b/, 'c' says /c/," just like in my video. Do not allow them to just say "/a/" when you show them a letter.

Activities to Teach Letters

22

Draw a letter on a piece of paper. Use something that represents that letter and glue it to the letter you drew. Cereal can be used for many letters. For example, if I am teaching the letter "a," I could use Apple Jacks to glue to the letter I wrote.

23

Use a sign language chart for them to sign the letter and sound out as well. This will connect to your kinesthetic child.

24

Use index cards to make capital letters (individually) and lowercase letters (individually). Play the match game. As your child flips each letter have them say the letter and their sound. You may only want to use a few sets of letters in the beginning. To offer support to new learners, you may use an alphabet chart for them to reference the correct sets.

25

Play bingo with the letters and sounds. You can buy a bingo game or make cards yourself. It can have four, six, eight, nine, or twelve squares. If your child is new to bingo, four squares might be enough.

26 ....

Use sand in a tray. If you don't have a tray, use a shoebox to let your child draw letters with their finger. Instead of sand, you can use sugar or salt or even dirt.

27 ....

Use clay to let your child mold the letters. This also helps with hand-eye coordination and fine motor skills.

Fine motor skills are the coordination of small muscles in movement with eyes, usually involving the synchronization of hands and fingers.

28 ....

Use pipe cleaners to let your child mold the letters. This also helps with fine motor skills.

29 ....

Sing "Old McDonald" song with the letters. "Old McDonald had farm, e, i, e, i, o, and on that farm, he had an a, e, i, e, i, o, with an /a/, /a/, here and an /a/, /a, there, here and /a/, there an /a/ every-where and /a/,/a/." Visit my YouTube video for an example of the song being song.

30 ....

Make another set of alphabet cards (using index cards) where the consonants are one color and the vowels (a, e, i, o, u) are red. Teach your child that vowels are special because every word has a vowel in it, even the words "a" and "i." Make sure to point this out in words everywhere by saying, "See, there are two vowels in Monday, an "o" and an "a." Point this out in their name or other words that are important and from the word wall. Do this with lots of words until they understand that it's not a word if they don't use a vowel. This will help them when it is time for them to write words. Check for understanding by asking them to identify the vowels in words.

31

To further help your child develop hand-eye coordination and build their ability to write letters, start your child out with drawing. Let them hold a pencil and draw whatever their hands can. Place tools in their hands often with which they may draw, write, or paint.

32

Once they are able, teach them to draw lines—all kinds of lines—vertical, horizontal, zigzag, squiggly, circles, squares, triangles, etc. Show them how they can use these lines and shapes to draw simple pictures.

33

Once they are able, teach them to use the dry erase board to have them write letters.

34

Allow your learner to use chart paper to draw letters.

35 ....

Let them use paint, crayons, colored pencils, colored pens, and chalk to draw letters.

36 ....

Ask your child to draw the letter ___. At first, they may need the picture letter chart.

37 ....

Once your child can identify letters and knows the sounds, you can have them use a dry erase board to write the letter that says /k/ or the letter that says /p/. This is a way to assess your child's progress and to help them learn how to build sounds to make words later.

Blending sounds to make words is the decoding part of reading. Once learners know sounds, they can blend them to make words. In this book, I only speak about the twenty-six sounds of the alphabet and the long vowel sounds. The English language has many more sounds.

38 ....

Once your child knows enough sounds, they can begin to blend. Knowing two sounds can be enough to blend. For example, you can have your child blend the sounds /i//t/. Ask them to read the word. Do that with as many words as you can: "am," "is," "an," "us," "if," and "in." Words like "me," and "we," use the vowels in a different way.

I wouldn't use these in the beginning. Although these are words that can be sounded out, they happen to be high-frequency words as well. High-frequency words are words found frequently in text.

39

Build up the word with three letters: /c//a//n/ or /b//i//g/. Find a list of phonetically spelled three-letter words online. You can also use the rhyming word lists as well. Most of them should be words you can sound out.

40

As your child learns words, add these words to the word wall. Use the word wall as much as possible. Use it to practice learning new words, and when your learner wants to write. Reference it as often as possible. You can play word games. I'll suggest some later. Make sure your learner adds these words to the wall themselves. Have them read those words randomly and often.

41

Words that your child cannot sound out are what some teachers refer to as "red" words. These are high-frequency words because they are seen most often in books. Teachers use Dolch or Fry lists to teach these words. No matter which you call them, they are often the same words just rearranged in a different order. You can Google the Dolch and Fry lists. You can ask your local school district which list they use and ask them to give you a copy. Teach these words three to five at a time. The next few ideas are for teaching high-frequency words. Put these words on index cards. Add these to your word wall.

Practicing High-Frequency Words

42

Say the word and spell out the word.

43

Say the word, spell out the word, and say the word again as you pat down your arm. Then slide your hand down at the end when you say the word for the final time. Do this five times for each word. Check out my YouTube channel for an example.

44

Have your child write these words in different ways.

45

Write each word three to five times each.

46

Step write the words. Start with the first letter on the top line and add a letter as you move down one line at a time. Do it backwards too!

Example:

t

th

the

47 ....

Rainbow write the words with each letter in a different color. For example, t, h, e.

48 ....

Use the words in a word search puzzle. You can use a hundred chart to make this.

49 ....

Use construction paper to make strips. Have your child write the words on the strips using finger spaces between each word. Have your child make a bracelet or necklace with the strips.

50 ....

Have your child make up a sentence for the word. Try to make them simple. Use words from your word wall. For example: "I like the cat." "The cat is brown." "You are a big red dog."

You can stretch sentences as your learners get comfortable with writing. They should know lots of sounds and be able to read some high-frequency words.

They don't always have to spell words correctly. We are not looking for perfection.

51

Model how to write sentences with your child. If they can give you a sentence using the high-frequency words, demonstrate how to write that sentence with them. This is a good time to have them copy the sentence after you have written it and then have them read it. Hang this on the wall somewhere so they can come back to it whenever they want. I like to do three to five sentences with a learner.

52

Use letter tiles to make words. You can make some paper tiles by using the hundreds sheets that you can find online for free or go to the website for Teachers Pay Teachers (www.teacherspayteachers.com). Add one letter to each box and you have tiles that can be cut and used to make words. You can also use this sheet to create a wordsearch.

53

Put sentences that you make with the red words on sentence strips. Have children read them. Then cut them up and put the sentence back in order, reading each word as they do so. Make sure to keep an original copy of the sentences.

54 ....

Have your child identify the high-frequency words in books. You can make this fun by using a small magnifying glass and they can pretend they are going on a hunt for words like an investigator.

55 ....

Have your child practice writing high-frequency words in the sand; use clay or pipe cleaners to form them; write them in the air, on the counter, on the floor, or on your back with their finger.

56 ....

Use decodable books to teach fluency. Fluency is the ability to read with speed, accuracy, and proper expression. Decodable books are simple stories that allow students to practice letter sounds and sounds of words as well as the high-frequency words. So, these books will have words in them that you can't sound out such as "the" and "was" and they will have words that can be decoded such as "cat," "dog," or "mom." You may be able to find them at the local library.

57 ....

Use leveled readers to teach comprehension. Leveled readers are books arranged in order from easy to hard. There are several ways to determine your child's reading level through a reading diagnostic test. There are several reading assessment tools that school districts may use to determine a student's reading level.

Some examples include: Lexile Analyzer, Guided Reading, Developmental Reading Assessment (DRA), and Reading Maturity Metric. Ask your child's school district which one they use and which level your child is on. You can also get a reading diagnostic by going to: www.purposefuleducations.com.

Your local library should have leveled readers in their children's department; if they don't, you could ask them to order some.

Reading diagnostics measure a student's abilities in five components of reading: phonemic awareness, phonics, vocabulary, fluency, and comprehension. Students read a timed passage, while the teachers follow a series of codes to record if the child has missed, mispronounced, added, or didn't recognize words. It is a word-by-word recording called a running record. They may also ask comprehension questions, and complete tasks such as spelling words or reading a list of words. Simply put, students are leveled according to the story they can read with some mistakes. This is what teachers generally call a student's instructional level. This is the level at which they need assistance.

58

Use the leveled readers and copy pages or if the book has one sentence on each page, write the sentences and have your child put them back in order using the book to reference. Your child should look at the sentence you wrote and compare it against the sentence in the story.

59 ....

Here are a few ideas you can use for playing games with the word wall. First, children love the word wall. It is a place where they can add the words they know. They are the master of the wall because they will master this wall.

Here are a few games:

- *Read the Words:* "Read the words under letters 'c' and 'k.'" (Of course, you can choose how many words they read and which ones, or you can allow them to choose.)
- *I Spy:* For example, "I spy a word that has four letters and means one more than three."
- *Rhymes:* "This word rhymes with four." Allow them to choose all the words on the board that will rhyme.
- *Opposites:* "This word is the opposite of 'in.'"
- *Alphabetical Order:* "Take all the words from any list and put them in A-B-C order."

60 ....

Use picture books to have your child make up stories. This helps with speaking and listening skills. It also provides practice using imagination for writing, teaches how to sequence a story, and so much more. Record these stories and let your learner listen to them.

61

You can have them write a story. Revise and edit the story to make it better.

Writing sentences with your learner has multiple benefits.

- The words they are learning become more relevant in everyday life. Point this out during the day when you are not in a learning mode.
- They can read and write them to convey a message. This is a lesson they will need in school and in real life.
- We read and write from left to right.
- It teaches that capital letters are used at the beginning of sentences; how to use punctuation; and how to put spaces between the words.
- It teaches them the formation of letters and how to write them properly.
- It teaches them penmanship.
- The reason it is presented here is to practice the words in a way that is fun, relevant, and helps your learner retain the words being taught, which is what you want!

62

Have your learner use a journal to write daily. You can search Google for topics appropriate for your child's age. Even if your child cannot write, they can draw pictures of their days or how they feel. They can draw a sequence of pictures showing what happened in the morning, the afternoon, or in the evening. They can share this with you and other family members. Drawing pictures leads to writing words and then sentences.

Use Index Cards

63 ....

Use index cards to write numbers on one card and the word for the number on another. Match them.

64 ....

Do the same with color words. Use an index card to draw a picture with the color on one and then print the name of the color on the other. Match them.

65 ....

Use sheets from a coloring book. Write numbers in the empty areas of the coloring sheet. At the bottom of the coloring sheet, write the number and the color you want them to color the number. Have students look for the color word on the crayon. In the beginning you may also have to color the word at the bottom for support. Use only Crayola crayons. They show real colors. Start with the basic eight colors.

Calendar Activities

66 ....

The next set of activities can be used for calendar ideas and will teach your child number literacy in a way that will be fun, and they will retain the information. The most important part of calendar is doing it consistently and making it interactive.

There are a slew of activities that you can find on Google. Search "second grade calendar activities." Teachers use these activities in their classrooms all the time. As your learner grows, so can the activities within the calendar.

65

I use the calendar as one of the ways to introduce rhyming words through poetry. For young children, poetry is fun. They can memorize poems if they hear them enough, which is why consistency is important. Each month I introduce a new poem from *Chicken Soup with Rice: A Book of Months* by Maurice Sendak. I introduce the book by saying the title of the poem and the author's name. I read it a couple of times. Then I read it and the learners repeat it a couple of times. It may be hard for them to repeat it at first. Be consistent and they will know it by heart by the end of the month. Have them pronounce the words clearly. Make sure to point to each word as you are reading. You should come back to this poem at least two to three times a week, if you're homeschooling every day. After the third week or so, your learner should be able to repeat you well and should be ready to do some activities with the poem.

Here are some activities:
- Point to the title of the poem
- Find that word (January) in the poem
- Listen for the rhyming words in the poem. Circle them.
- Identify the words that you may have studied this week or previously.

66

I use the monthly poem as an opportunity to discuss the seasons and weather in each month. I have my learners draw a picture of what they can do outside, a holiday that is happening, and anything else special that happens in that month each year. Pictures are the beginning of writing. Children should learn to draw pictures with details. Take time to teach them to draw pictures. Simple pictures can be drawn with the shapes such as circles, triangles, rectangles, straight lines, or squiggly lines. Use YouTube to find easy drawings of people, animals, and places.

67

Write a letter to your child each time you meet for learning. If you're homeschooling, do this daily. This is going to teach letter writing, reinforce days of the week and months of the year and show written words. It will reinforce right to left coordination, finger spacing, and punctuation, and you can even use it to intro-duce spelling words correctly.

Letters have five parts: heading, greeting, body, closing, and signature. The heading is the date. I usually do this in long form until I have taught them the short form. The greeting can be "Hello" or "Dear." It addresses the person reading the letter. The body is the message you want to relay. The closing is your way of saying goodbye. It can be said many ways; some of the most popular are: "Love," "Thank You," or "Sincerely." Whichever you use, remember it is the closing and should be capitalized. Finally, the signature is the name of the person who is writing the letter. It may say Miss

Tissua, or Mom. Again, make sure it is capitalized. This will teach them how to read, and build fluency and their confidence. At first, they will just be reading from memory so you should start the sentence the same most times. I change the beginning, of the letter some but I always begin with "Today is (and add the day)." "It is (Month, day and year)." Then I may switch up the body, remembering to use the words that I have taught them. If students do different activities on different days of the week, this is where I would differentiate the letter.

For example:
Dear Leah,
Today is Monday. It is February 5, 2021. Today we will learn the letter /a/. We will have gym today.
Love, Dad

Keep it simple and add to it as your child learns to read fluently by themselves.

As your learner learns and grows, this letter evolves. The letter can become a place where you practice revision and editing. This is the process of making their writing better. It is an important and sometimes challenging task for some learners. Once your learner knows the rules for writing a letter you may make mistakes in the letter, like starting a sentence with a lowercase word, misspelling their names, or leaving off punctuation. You can start by telling them that there are some mistakes, or there are three mistakes, or some children may recognize it on their own.

68

Have them write you a letter back. Write it together first—maybe for Mother's Day or Father's Day or on your birthday. If your learner can't write yet, have them draw pictures and label them.

69

Leave notes and letters around the house or in your child's lunch bag or overnight bag if they go to stay at someone's house. Make them simple. For example: "Have a good day!" or "I love you."

Reading and Writing Practice

70

Talk to your child. I can't stress this one enough. This develops oral language, speaking and listening skills, vocabulary, and it gives them the words to use when they speak to others. Give them multiple tasks to do at one time. See if they can do them without coming back for more direction.

71

Write the room or house! Have your child walk around the room or house finding words they know and writing them on a notepad, dry erase board, or paper attached to clipboard. Clipboards make them feel important. Only allow them to write the words they know. Ask them to bring them back to you and read their list. If they don't know the word, they often know where they got the word. Ask them to point that out; they may be able to remember the word. Remind them to write only words they know. They will write that word again and eventually it will become a word they know. In this activity, your child is learning to write words and read them.

72

Record your child reading and have them listen to it.

73

Record stories for your child to read or go to my YouTube page and subscribe to listen to stories.

74

Record yourself reading a story and send it to your child.

75

Record a story and let your learner read it with the book.

76

Use the word wall to help write stories. It's been my experience that stories are more detailed when they are true stories. Most writers are extremely creative and use much of their real-life experiences to make stories come alive.

77 ....

Teach your child to print their name, first and last. They may have to begin by tracing their name before they can write it on their own. To get a tracing of your name, search Google for free name tracing. Teach your child all the letters in their name. Make sure they know which letter is first, and which is last. Make sure they understand which is capital and lowercase.

78 ....

Teach your child full names for the members of your family. Write them on paper and use them on index cards to assess if they can recognize important names in the family. Add these words to the word wall. This is good for safety.

79 ....

Teach your child their address and phone number. You can have them trace this, but this should be something hanging in their room all the time and you should go over it often.

80 ....

Start writing by teaching your child how to draw pictures and label the pictures. One of my favorite pictures to draw with learners is a self-portrait. It shows how they see themselves. Let your child look in a mirror and draw a picture of themselves and label it with their name.

81

Ask them to draw a picture of their family and label it. Later they can add simple sentences.

82

Have them draw pictures of holidays, birthdays, vacations, shopping trips, etc. Label these pictures and begin to write simple sentences. For example, on their birthday, they may draw a picture of themselves, the birthday cake, their favorite presents, and other guests at the party. Try to get them to draw as much detail as possible. Add words, like: "My birthday was fun." "I got a doll." "The cake was good." Make these sentences simple. At first, they may have to trace and copy your words so write together. Teachers call this scaffolding.

83

When writing with your child remember to speak the words out loud. Ask your child how to spell a word. If they don't know, they can reference the word wall, if the word is there. If not, you can begin to sound it out with them. Remember, we are not going for perfection. Sometimes I pause and let them know that the English language is "tricky." All words cannot be sounded out. High-frequency words cannot be sounded out. You can try to teach words by pattern or rhyming but rhyming words don't always make the same pattern. You can teach "my" with words like "by," "cry," "why," and "shy." These can all be added to the word wall.

84 ....

Let your child trace your sentences.

85 ....

Teach your child compound words. Compound words are two words put together to make one word. You can buy a game from the teachers' store, find something online, or you can write the words on index cards and find pictures online to match or you can have the kids draw their own. This is the best way to retain the information.

I would use three index cards for this activity. For this example, one would show the compound word "doghouse" with a picture of a doghouse. The second one would show "dog" with a picture of a dog and the third would show "house" with a picture of a house. Use the first picture of the doghouse to support students finding the other two pieces. Later you can ask them to put the words together without the first picture.

I like to make a small book with compound words too. I use a piece of paper folded in half. On the front, we write the word "doghouse" and draw a picture. Inside we draw the picture of the dog on one side and a house on the other. Make sentences using the compound words. Read them often. Hang them around the room.

86 ....

Teach your child about homophones. Homophones are words that sound the same but are spelled differently. Use two index cards for this activity. Write one word with corresponding picture on one card and the other word and picture on the second card. Play the matching game.

For example: "I" and "eye".

Eventually, you can take away the pictures but support learning with the original list of the homophones.

87 ....

Teach your child about synonyms. Synonyms are words that mean the same thing.

88 ....

Teach your child about antonyms. Antonyms are words that are opposites.

89 ....

Practice homophones, synonyms, and antonyms by using picture cards to play a matching game.

90 ....

Teach your child nouns, pronouns, and proper nouns. Nouns names a person, place, or thing. Pronouns take the place of a noun in a sentence. Proper nouns name a particular person, place, or thing. Use a chart to demonstrate the differences. For example: girl, her, Sheila.

91

Teach your child verbs. Verbs are action words. They are things you can do, like run, draw, blink, or snore.

92

Teach your child adjectives. An adjective describes a noun such as big, tall, six, yellow. All number words and color words are adjectives.

93

Play word bingo.

94

Play picture bingo.

95

Play rhyming bingo.

96

Make the bingo games yourself.

97

Play Hangman with words.

98

Draw a mountain on a white piece of typing paper. Add sight words going up the mountain. Have your learner read the sight words. If they miss a word, they have to go back down the mountain to start all over again. Do this until they have mastered all the words along the mountain. I call this *Over the Mountain*.

99

In education we sometimes say you learn everything you need to learn in kindergarten. I believe I have covered all the kindergarten literacy standards in this book. However, I would start these activities with my child as soon as possible, singing alphabet songs and reading stories as soon as I found out I was pregnant. All activities in this book will set the foundation for reading. If you are successful with these strategies your child should be able to decode words and read high-frequency words with fluency.

100

Read, read, and keep reading.

Below you will find the Michigan State Standards for Kindergarten.

FOR LITERATURE

Key ideas and details

- With prompting and support ask and answer questions about key details in a text.
- With prompting and support retell familiar stories, including key details.
- With prompting and support, identify characters, settings, and major events in a story.

Craft and structure

- Ask and answer questions about unknown words in text.
- Recognize common types of text (storybooks, poems, etc.)
- With prompting and support, identify the author and illustrator of a story and define the role of each in the telling of the story.

Integration of Knowledge and Ideas

- With prompting and support, describe the relationship between illustrations and the story which they appear (i.e. what moment in a story the illustration depicts)
- With prompting and support, compare and contrast the theme, setting, and plots of stories written by the same authors about the same similar characters (i.e. in books of a series.)

Range of Reading and Level of Complexity

- By the end of the year, read and comprehend literature, including stories, dramas, and poems, at the high-end of grades 2-3 text complexity band independently and proficiently.

STANDARDS FOR INFORMATIONAL TEXT
Key ideas and details

- With prompting and support ask and answer questions about key details in a text.
- With prompting and support, identify main topic and retell key details of a text.
- With prompting and support describe the connections between two individuals, events, ideas, or pieces of information in a text.

Craft and structure

- Ask and answer questions about unknown words in text.
- Identify the front and back cover and the title page of the book.
- Identify the author and illustrator of a text and define the role of each in presenting the ideas or information in a text.

Integration of Knowledge and Ideas

- With prompting and support, describe the relationship between illustrations and the context in which they appear (e.g. what person, place, thing, or idea in a text an illustration depicts)

- With prompting and support, identify the reason an author gives support points in a text.
- With prompting and support, identify basic similarities and differences between two texts on the same topic (e.g., illustrations, descriptions, or procedures).

RANGE OF READING AND LEVEL OF COMPLEXITY

Actively engage in group reading activities with purpose and understanding.

Print Concepts

Demonstrate understanding of the organization and basic features of print.

- Follow words from left to right, top to bottom, and page by page.
- Recognize that spoken words are represented in written language by specific sequences of letters.
- Recognize that words are separated by spaces in print.
- Recognize and name all uppercase and lowercase alphabet.

Phonological Awareness

Demonstrate understanding of spoken words, syllables, and sounds (phonemes)

- Recognize and produce rhyming words.
- Count, pronounce, blend, and segment syllables in spoken words.
- Blend and segment onsets and rhymes in spoken words.

- Isolate and pronounce initial, medial vowels, and finals sounds (phonemes) in three phonemes (consonant, vowel, consonant or CVC words). This does not include CVC's ending in /l/, /r/, or /x/.
- Add or substitute individual sounds (phonemes) in simple, one-syllable words to make new words.

Phonics and Word Recognition

Know and apply grade-level phonics and word analysis skills and decoding words.

- Demonstrate basic knowledge of one-to-one letter-sound correspondences by producing the primary sound or many of the most frequent sounds for each consonants.
- Associate all the long and short sounds with common sounds (graphemes) for the five major vowels.
- Read common high-frequency words by sight (e.g. the, of, to, you, she, my, is, are, do, does).
- Distinguish between similarly spelled words by identifying the sounds of the letters that differ.

Fluency

Read emergent-reader text with purpose and understanding.

WRITING

Types of Purposes

- Use a combination of drawing, dictating, and writing to compose opinion pieces in which they tell a reader the topic or the name of the book they are writing about and state an opinion or preference about the topic or book (i.e., "My favorite book is...").

- Use a combination of drawing, dictating, and writing to compose an informative/explanatory text in which they name what they are writing about and supply some information about the topic.

- Use a combination of drawing, dictating, and writing to narrate a single event or several loosely linked events, talk about the events in order, in which they occurred, and provide a reaction to what happened.

Production and Distribution of Writing

- NOT for kindergartners

- With guidance and support from adults, respond to questions and suggestions from peers, and add details to strengthen writing as needed.

- With guidance and support from adults, explore a variety of digital tools to produce and publish writing, including in collaboration with peers.

Research to Build and Present Knowledge

- Participate in shared research and writing projects (e.g. explore several books by favorite author and express opinions about them)
- With guidance and support from adult, recall information from experiences or gather information from provided sources to answer a question.

SPEAKING AND LISTENING

Communication and Collaboration

- Participate in collaborative conversation with diverse partners about kindergarten topics and text with peers and adults in small and large groups.
  - » Follow agreed upon rules for discussion (e.g., listening to others and taking turn speaking about topics and texts under discussion)
  - » Continue a conversation through multiple exchanges.
- Confirm understanding of a text read aloud or information presented orally or through media by asking questions about key details and requesting clarification if something is not understood.
- Ask and answer questions to seek help, get information, or clarify something that is not understood.

Presentation of Knowledge and Ideas
- Describe familiar people, places, things, and events, and with promoting and support, provide additional details.
- Add drawings or other visual displays to descriptions as desired to provide additional details.
- Speak audibly and express thoughts, feelings, and ideas clearly.

LANGUAGE

Conventions of Standard English
- Demonstrate command of conventions of standard English grammar and usage when writing and speaking.
  » Print many uppercase and lowercase letters.
  » Use frequently occurring nouns and verbs.
  » Form regular and plural orally by adding /s/ or /es/ (e.g. dog, dogs, wish, wishes)
  » Understand and use question words (interrogatives) (e.g., who, what, when, why, where, how).
  » Use the most frequently occurring prepositions (e.g., to, from, in, out, off, for, of, by, with)
  » Produce and expand complete sentences in shared language activities.
- Demonstrate command of the conventions of standard English capitalization, punctuation, and spelling when writing.

> » Capitalize the first letter in a sentence, and I.
> » Recognize and name end punctuation.
> » Write a letter or letters for most consonants and short vowel sounds (phonemes).
> » Spell simple words phonetically, drawing on knowledge of letter-sound relationships.

Knowledge of Language

- Now applicable
- Determine and clarify the meaning of unknown multiple-meaning words and phrases based on kindergarten reading and content.
  > » Identify new meanings for familiar words and apply them accurately (e.g. knowing that a duck is a bird and learning the verb to duck).
  > » Uses the most frequently occurring inflections and affixes (e.g., -ed, -s, re-, un-, pre-, -ful, -less) as a clue to the meaning of an unknown word.
- With guidance and support from an adults, explore word relationships and nuances in word meanings.
  > » Sort common objects into categories (e.g., shapes, foods) to gain a sense of the concepts the categories represent.
  > » Demonstrate understandings of frequently occurring verbs and adjectives by relating them to their opposites (antonyms).

» Identify real world connections between words and their use (e.g., note places at school that are colorful).

» Distinguish shades of meaning among verbs describing the same general action (e.g., walk, march, strut, prance) by acting out meanings.

- Use words and phrases acquired through conversations, reading, and being read to, and responding to texts.

TYPE OF TEXTS OR GENRES

- **Stories:** children's adventure stories, folktales, legends, fables, fantasy, realistic fiction, and myth
- **Dialogue:** plays
- **Poetry:** include nursery rhymes and the subgenres of the narrative poem limerick and free verse poems
- **Literary nonfiction and historical, scientific, and technical text:** Include biographies and autobiographies; books about history, social studies, science, and the arts; technical texts, including directions, forms and information displayed in graphs, charts, or maps; digital sources and a range of topics.

Kindergarten books for text complexity

- *Over in the Meadow* by John Langstaff (traditional) (c1800)*
- *A Boy, a Dog, and a Frog* by Mercer Mayer (1967)
- *Pancakes for Breakfast* by Tomie DePaola (1978)
- *A Story, A Story* by Gail E. Haley (1970)*
- *Kitten's First Full Moon* by Kevin Henkes (2004)*
- *My Five Senses* by Aliki (1962)**
- *Truck* by Donald Crews (1980)
- *I Read Signs* by Tana Hoban (1987)
- *What Do You Do With a Tail Like This?* by Steve Jenkins and Robin Page (2003)*
- *Amazing Whales!* by Sarah L. Thomson (2005)*

Second grade books for text complexity

- *Mix a Pancake* by Christina G. Rossetti (1893)**
- *Mr. Popper's Penguins* by Richard Atwater (1938)*
- *Little Bear* by Else Holmelund Minarik, illustrated by Maurice Sendak (1957)**
- *Frog and Toad Together* by Arnold Lobel (1971)**
- *Hi! Fly Guy* by Tedd Arnold (2006)
- *A Tree Is a Plant* by Clyde Robert Bulla, illustrated by Stacey Schuett (1960)**
- *Starfish* by Edith Thacher Hurd (1962)
- *Follow the Water from Brook to Ocean* by Arthur Dorros (1991)**
- *From Seed to Pumpkin* by Wendy Pfeffer, illustrated by James Graham Hale (2004)*
- *How People Learned to Fly* by Fran Hodgkins and True Kelley (2007)*

ABOUT THE AUTHOR

Tissua Sherie Franklin was born to teenage parents in the small city of Hamtramck nestled in the middle of Detroit. She grew up with absentee parents, and there were few books being read to her as a child.

Poor, Black, and labeled as "at risk," she overcame great odds to attend Michigan State University and went on to dedicate her life to educating youth and families. She has a bachelor's degree in elementary education with minors in both English and business administration. She also has a master's degree in education leadership and administration and an education specialist degree in curriculum and instruction.

Her extensive education prepared her for teaching in the exceedingly multilingual city of Hamtramck, and her commitment to language education has taken her all the way to Dubai to work with Arabic-speaking students and staff.

As a reading specialist, writing department chair, instructor of K-12 students and parents, homeschool manager, and professional development instructor, Tissua knows how to teach reading to bilingual, special education, general education, and gifted students.

She contributes the success of her two sons, who both had early reading difficulties, to strong family values in which faith, purpose, integrity, and hard work set the foundation for success.

Most importantly, Tissua believes education is the vehicle through which equality travels.

Tissua Sherie Franklin EdS
Reading Specialist
Writing Specialist
Curriculum Specialist
Children Advocate
Mother
Auntie Tish

Made in United States
Orlando, FL
31 March 2024

45306624R00036